BILLY JOEL

FOR HARP

ARRANGED BY EMILY BRECKER

Dedicated to my brothers, jazz artists
Michael and Randy Brecker

ISBN 978-1-4803-4202-6

HAL•LEONARD®
CORPORATION
7777 W. BLUEMOUND RD. P.O. BOX 13819 MILWAUKEE, WI 53213

In Australia Contact:
Hal Leonard Australia Pty. Ltd.
4 Lentara Court
Cheltenham, Victoria, 3192 Australia
Email: ausadmin@halleonard.com.au

Visit Hal Leonard Online at
www.halleonard.com

ABOUT THIS BOOK

These arrangements for harp duplicate as closely as possible Billy Joel's original songs, as he performed them on his albums.

There are two versions of each title: The first is for pedal harps and large lever harps tuned to E-flat. These arrangements are at the intermediate/advanced level. The second version is for small lever harps tuned to C (in most songs) but can be played on any harp. These arrangements are at the beginner/intermediate level and contain few, if any, lever changes. There are more specific tuning instructions for lever harps in the top left corner of some arrangements. Lever changes are shown with diamond note heads. Pedal markings are located below the bass staff.

I would like to thank the following people for their generosity with this project: Jeffrey Schroedl and Marina Belica (for making it happen); harpist/teacher/mentor Mindy Cutcher (*beyond all words…*); harpists Kathy DeAngelo, Gráinne Hambly, Maeve Gilchrist, and Leslie Stickley (my musical inspirations, who planted the seeds); dear husband Howard Greenberg and my family (for unwavering support); daughter Sarah (for her keen ears); daughter-in-law Stephanie (for her graphics talent); Alex Posmontier (for his amazing musical and technical assistance); Arlene Gettlin/Myrna Marcus (the positive angels on my shoulders); pianist/teacher/second mother May K. Harrow (for her love, caring, and expert training); and my parents Ticky and Bob Brecker (where it all began).

Emily Brecker
April, 2013

CONTENTS

KEY TO SYMBOLS AND ABBREVIATIONS

This lists many of the symbols and abbreviations used in this book. Common musical symbols and abbreviations have been excluded.

Rolled chord: arpeggiate the chord from bottom to top.

l.h. Play with the *left hand.*

r.h. Play with the *right hand.*

• Get off the string quickly.

gliss. Glissando: a rapid scale played by sliding a second finger between two indicated notes.

Tap the rhythm on the sound board with fingers or knuckles.

Muffle the bass strings.

Muffle all of the strings.

L.V. An abbreviation for *let vibrate.*

∧ Used to point out the melody.

1 1 Slide the finger shown from the first string to the next.

+ Play with a flat thumb and open hand.

4 3 2 1 Pre-place the fingers as shown.

P.D.L.T. An abbreviation for *pres de la table.* Play very close to the soundboard to produce a dry, guitar-like effect.

And So It Goes

Words and Music by BILLY JOEL
Arranged by Emily Brecker

8

And So It Goes

For Small (and All) Harps

Words and Music by BILLY JOEL
Arranged by Emily Brecker

Slow Ballad, with rubato
Intro

Verse

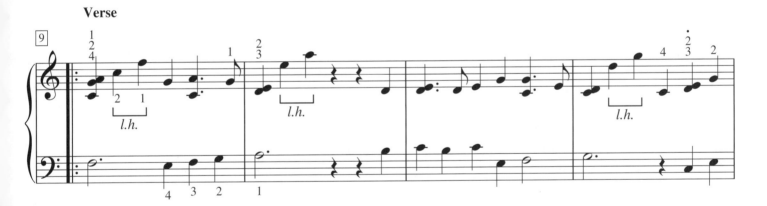

10

Bridge

Verse

Bridge

38

42 **Verse**

46

50

54 **Ending**

Don't Ask Me Why

Words and Music by BILLY JOEL
Arranged by Emily Brecker

Lever Harps: Begin
with middle D sharped

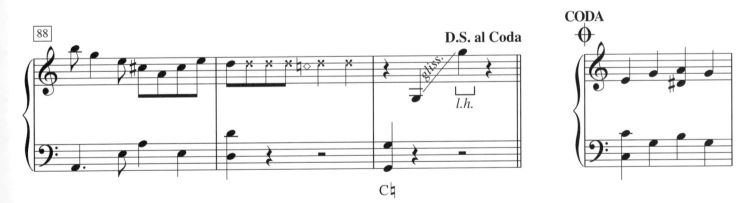

Don't Ask Me Why
For Small (and All) Harps

Words and Music by BILLY JOEL
Arranged by Emily Brecker

Lever Harps: Begin
with middle D sharped

Moderately

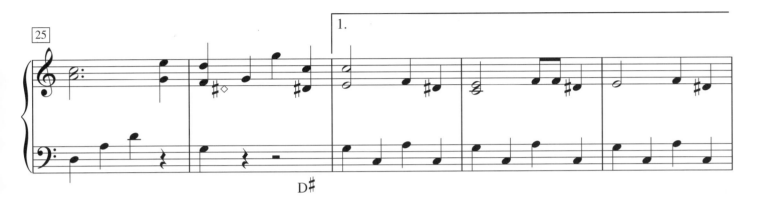

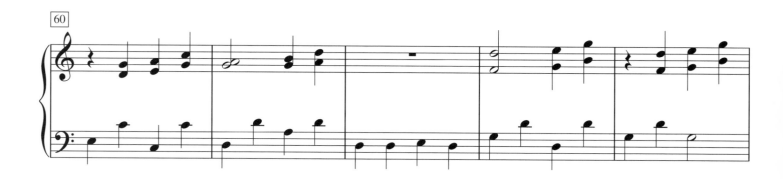

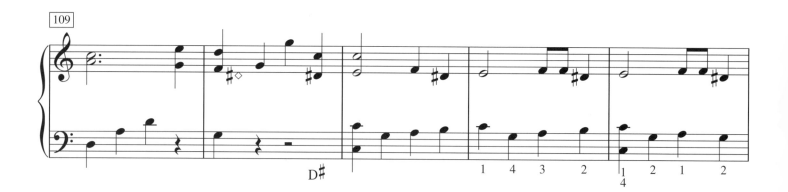

Honesty

Words and Music by BILLY JOEL
Arranged by Emily Brecker

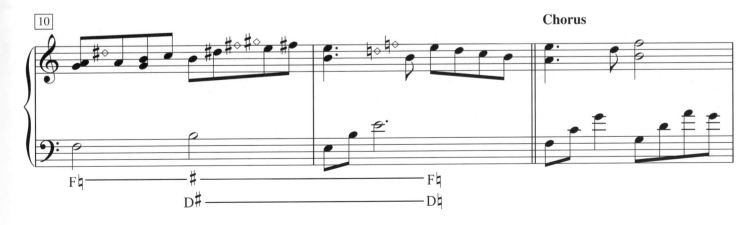

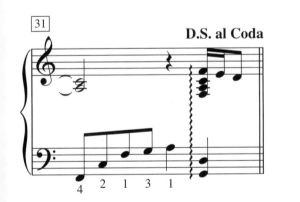

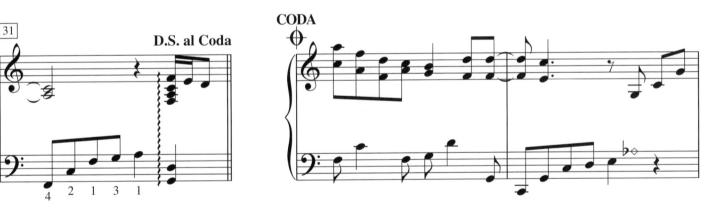

Honesty

For Small (and All) Harps

Words and Music by BILLY JOEL
Arranged by Emily Brecker

I've Loved These Days

Words and Music by BILLY JOEL
Arranged by Emily Brecker

Slowly, regally

𝄋 (Final Verse)

F#

Bb

F♮

To Coda ⊕

B♮

1.

2.

1

F#

I've Loved These Days

For Small (and All) Harps

Words and Music by BILLY JOEL
Arranged by Emily Brecker

Slowly, regally

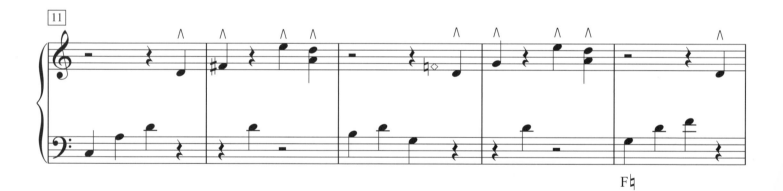

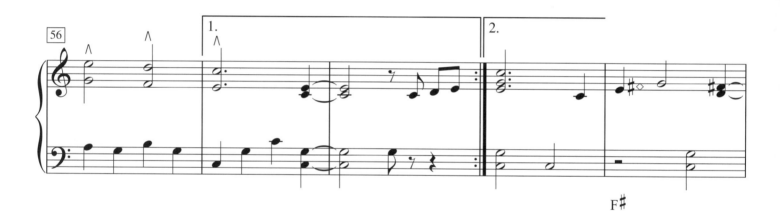

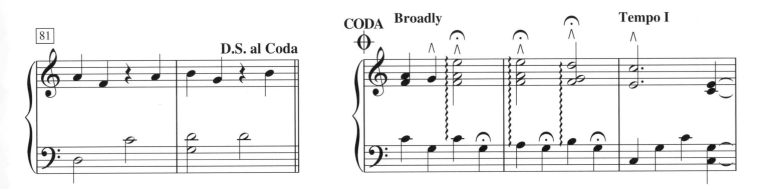

An Innocent Man

Words and Music by BILLY JOEL
Arranged by Emily Brecker

Moderate Caribbean feel

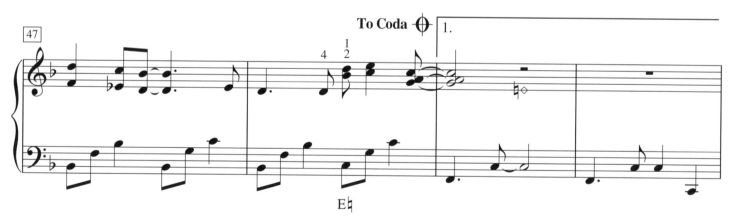

fade away

An Innocent Man
For Small (and All) Harps

Words and Music by BILLY JOEL
Arranged by Emily Brecker

Lever Harps: Tune the B
above middle C to B-flat.
Begin with that lever
in the UP position.

Moderate Caribbean feel

Bb

Bb

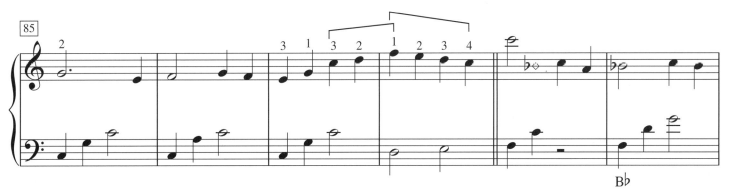

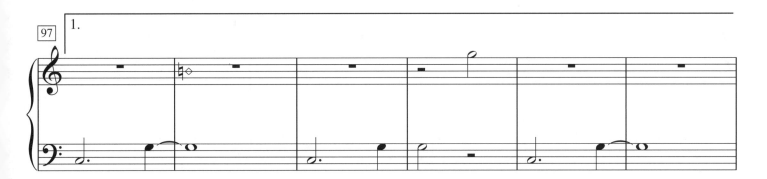

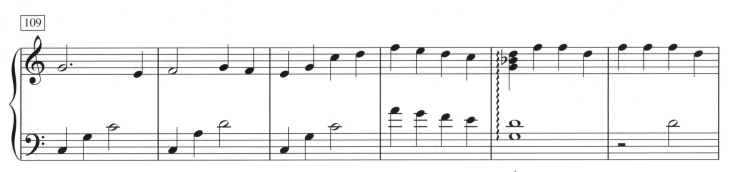

115

121

D.S. al Coda

CODA

B♮

127

133

pp

139

fade away

The Longest Time

Words and Music by BILLY JOEL
Arranged by Emily Brecker

Brightly, with a Doo-Wop "Oldies" sound

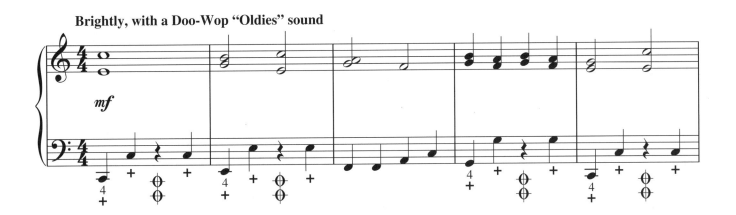

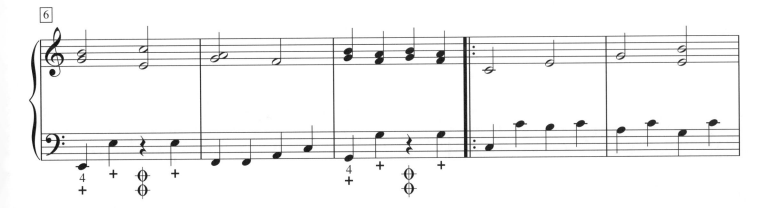

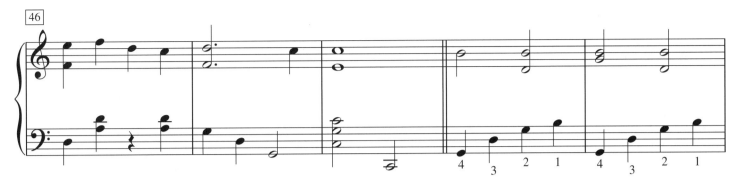

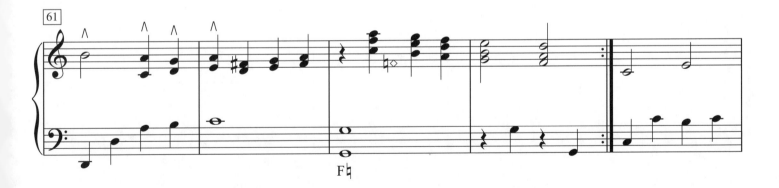

The Longest Time

For Small (and All) Harps

Words and Music by BILLY JOEL
Arranged by Emily Brecker

Brightly, with a Doo-Wop "Oldies" sound

*Cue notes are optional

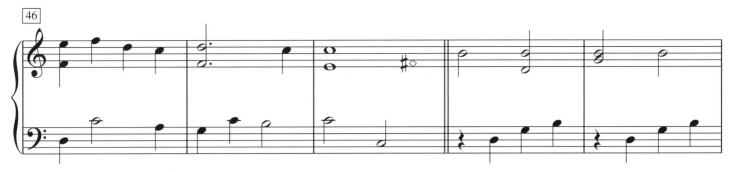

F#

F♮

Piano Man

Words and Music by BILLY JOEL
Arranged by Emily Brecker

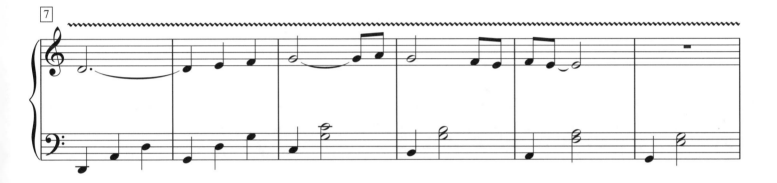

Refrain

143

149

**Jump to Refrain,   Verse 3
bar 211, on D.S.**

154

160

166

P.D.L.T.

Refrain

D.S. al Coda | **Optional Ending**

CODA

Piano Man
For Small (and All) Harps

Words and Music by BILLY JOEL
Arranged by Emily Brecker

Verse 1

P.D.L.T.

61

52

58

64

70

76
Refrain

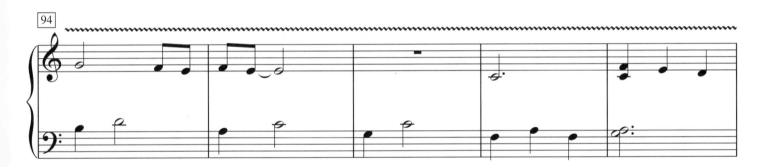

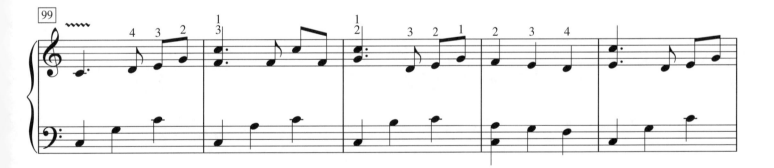

She's Got a Way

Words and Music by BILLY JOEL
Arranged by Emily Brecker

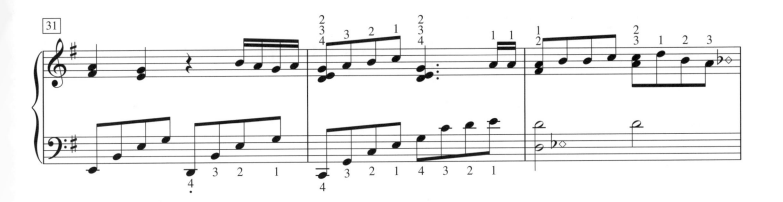

Bridge

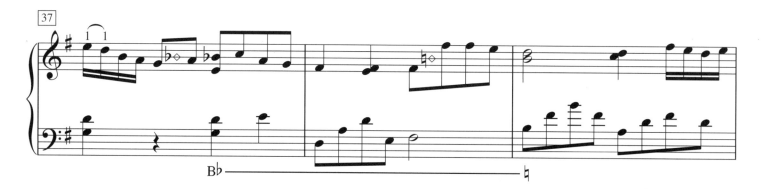

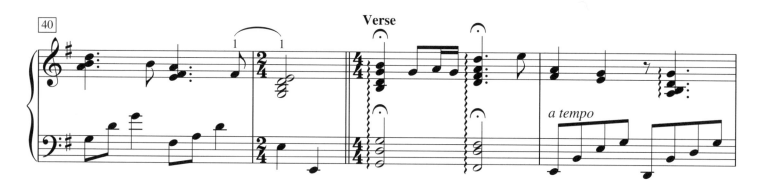

Verse

She's Got a Way

For Small (and All) Harps

Words and Music by BILLY JOEL
Arranged by Emily Brecker

Lever Harps: Tune the B
above middle C to B-flat.
Begin with that lever
in the UP position.

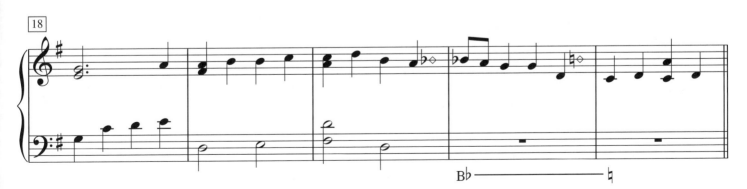

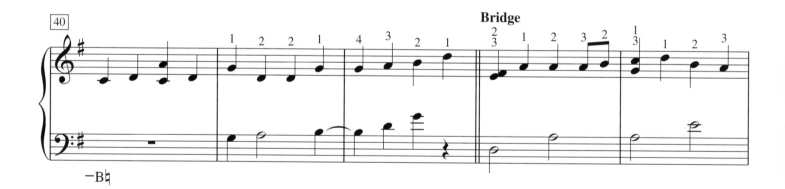

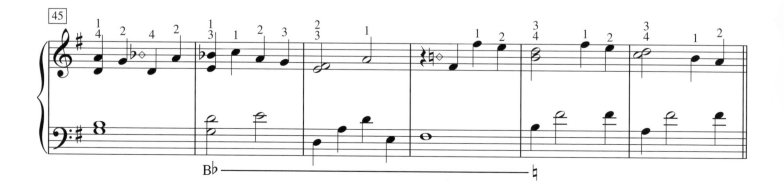

70

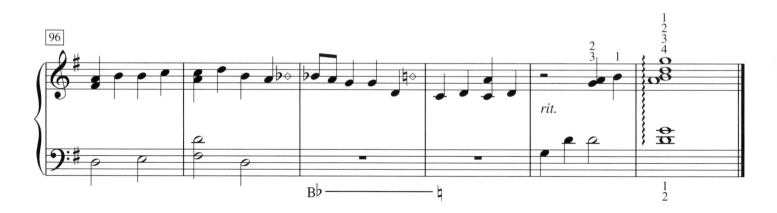

Summer, Highland Falls

Words and Music by BILLY JOEL
Arranged by Emily Brecker

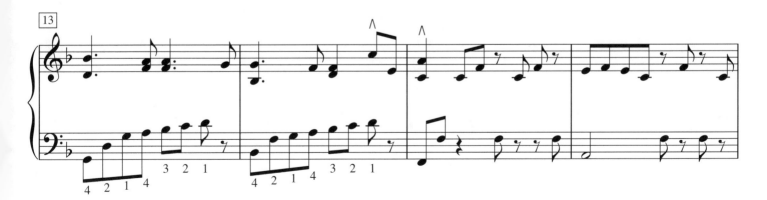

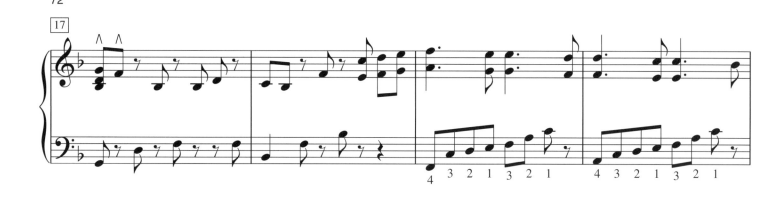

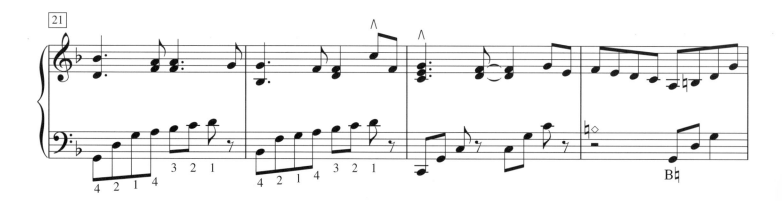

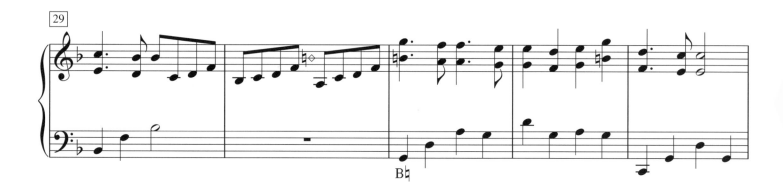

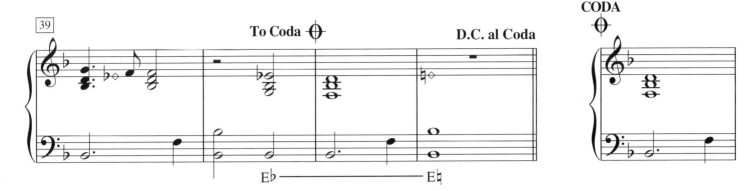

Summer, Highland Falls

For Small (and All) Harps

Words and Music by BILLY JOEL
Arranged by Emily Brecker

Lever Harps: Tune the B
above middle C to B-flat.
Begin with that lever
in the UP position.

Moderately
Intro

Verse

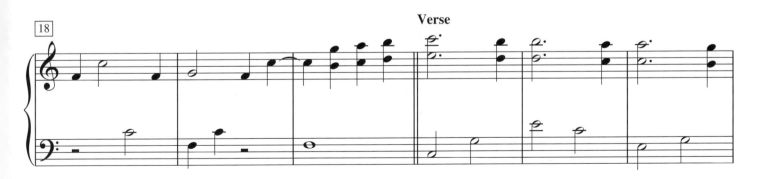

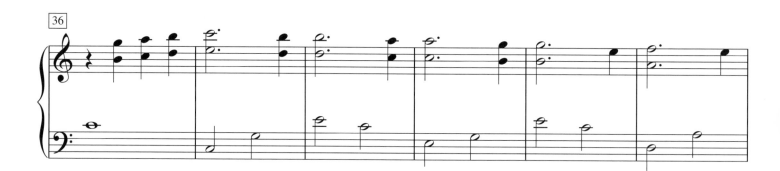

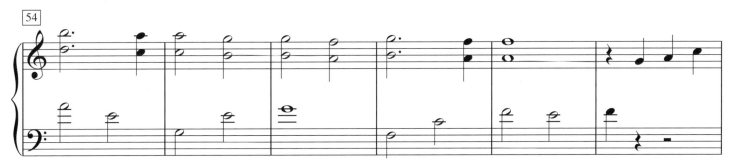

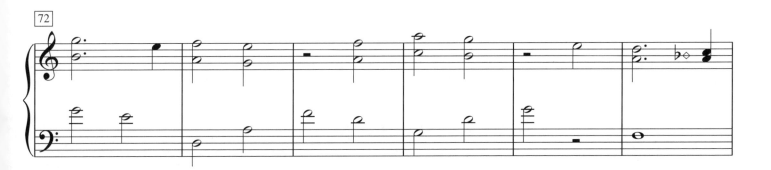

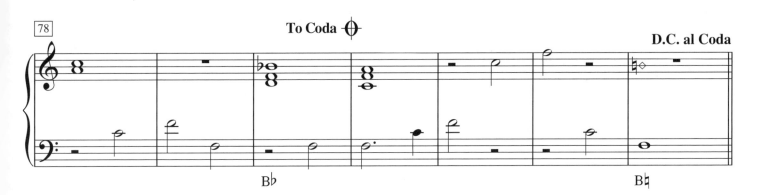

CODA

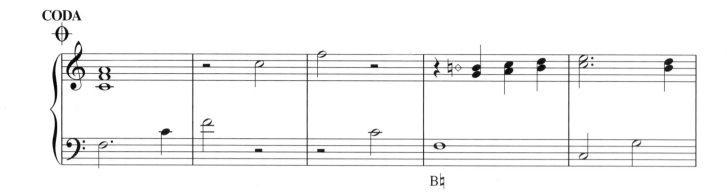

90

95

101

107

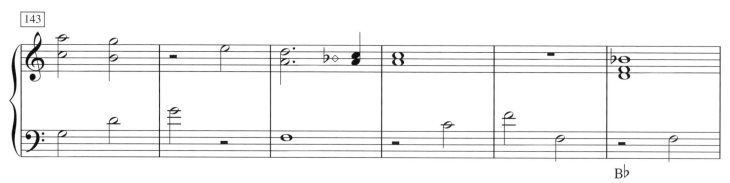

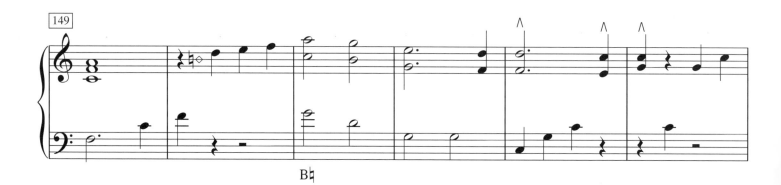

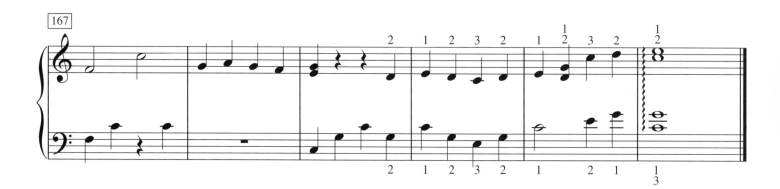

You're My Home

Words and Music by BILLY JOEL
Arranged by Emily Brecker

82

84

D.S. al Coda

CODA

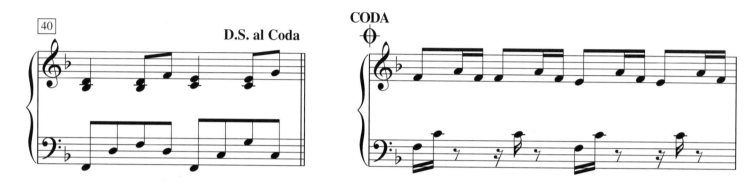

You're My Home

For Small (and All) Harps

Words and Music by BILLY JOEL
Arranged by Emily Brecker

Moderately

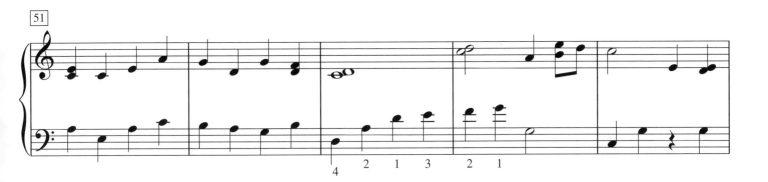

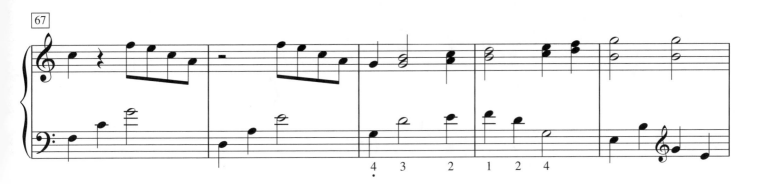

D.S. al Coda

CODA

*Cue notes are optional